Lisa D. Hoff

SANTA FE
NEW MEXICO

Sightseeing in 88 Pictures.

SANTA FE — PAST AND PRESENT

In the summer of 1598, a long train of wagons, pack animals, horses, cattle, sheep, goats, 129 soldier-settlers, their families, Indian servants, and eight Franciscan friars arrived at the upper Rio Grande to build the first permanent Spanish colony in New Mexico.

The first two settlements were not successful and, finally, decimated by starvation, desertion and Indian revolts, they were abandoned in favor of a new beginning on the banks of the Santa Fe River.

It was the second governor of the province, Don Pedro de Peralta, who established La Villa Real de Santa Fe (the Royal City of the Holy Faith) as the capital of Nuevo Mejico in 1610 under orders from Philip III of Spain.

Life remained precarious and rough for the colonists in the new location, but they gradually began to adapt to the environment, and giving up their dream of finding the legendary "Cities of Gold," they settled down to colonize the new province. Each family received two lots for a house and a garden, two neighboring fields to grow vegetables, two additional fields for growing vineyards and olives, and about 133 acres of land. In return for their land and water rights, settlers were obliged to live in the city for 10 consecutive years, to grow crops on their lands, to help maintain the "acequias" (irrigation canals), and to stand ready to serve as unpaid soldiers when necessary. Throughout the early 1600's, the colonial population of Santa Fe held steady at about 250 farmers, artisans, traders, missionaries and other frontiersmen, and 750 Indian servants. The settlers lived in flat adobe houses outside the enclosed plaza; the Indian servants lived in their own neighborhood across the Santa Fe River. The Plaza with its government houses (Casas Reales) at one end, and adobe church at the other, was the civil and spiritual center of the capital.

Although the King in Spain, the Viceroy in Mexico, and the Laws of the Indies, clearly intended to protect the Indians from abuse at the hands of the governors and settlers, they suffered under the sovereignty of the Spaniards. The Indians had to work for the settlers and the missionaries for little or no pay, they were often forbidden to practice their religions or live according to their traditions, and they had to pay tribute in corn, hides and blankets to the governor and to those settlers who had received a trusteeship over Indians as payment for their services to Spain. Indian resentment erupted in the Pueblo Revolt of 1680. The uprising ended with the Spaniards abandoning Santa Fe and New Mexico and retreating to El Paso, where they remained for the next 12 years.

In 1692, Diego de Vargas, the newly appointed governor of New Mexico, recaptured the city, and the following year, the settlers returned and started rebuilding Santa Fe.

The 1700's in Santa Fe saw only a few changes from the preceding century. People still bartered with chiles, corn, peas, sheep and other products and animals in exchange for services, goods and even lands - money was not introduced until the end of the century. The governor continued to quarrel with the friars and the cabildo (government), and Santa Feans kept on enjoying themselves at fiestas, fandangos (dances), and in gambling houses. They went to cock fights, to parades, watched the Indian dances in the Plaza or the dramatic presentations of historical and Biblical themes. The furnishings and decorations in homes were simple, and mostly made locally. Meals were cooked in the fireplace in heavy kettles or outside in "hornos," beehive-shaped adobe ovens, and were served on pottery made by the Pueblos.

After the Pueblo Revolt, the lives of the Indians improved somewhat, although the governors, the political officials in charge of the pueblos, and wealthy landowners still extracted harsh fees and fines in the form of produce and labor from them, but at least the government stopped to try to integrate them into Spanish society, and the church ignored the practice of pre-Christian rituals and ceremonies.

In 1821, a momentous change took place in Mexico which was to influence the future of all Spanish possessions in America. Mexico gained its independence from Spain. Gradually life in New Mexico began to change. With the new Mexican constitution came citizenship for Indians, free trade and free speech, the abolishment of the old Spanish caste system, and something New Mexicans had managed to circumvent for over 200 years: direct taxation.

In 1821, a trader from Franklin, Missouri, William Becknell, set out along old Indian trails and along the tracks made by mountain men with a string of pack mules loaded with dry goods. He arrived in Santa Fe three months later to the cheers of all Santa Fe who were eagerly waiting in the Plaza to buy his goods. In the years that followed, the trail to New Mexico became a major international thoroughfare. It was not long, however, before the Santa Fe market was saturated with goods, and soon some of the traders directed their freight wagons down the old Camino Real to Chihuahua City. Since each trader had to stop at the customs house in Santa Fe to pay duties on their freight, the city became the prosperous center of a lively trade in both directions. Some caravans had as many as 636 wagons, engaged 750 teamsters and drovers, and carried goods worth one million dollars. When they returned to Missouri they were loaded with Mexican silver bullions, furs, blankets and sheep fleeces.

In 1846, Congress declared war on Mexico in order to clarify their long dispute over the boundary line between Texas and Mexico, and the status of Texas, which had been admitted to the Union in 1845, even though Mexico still considered it one of their districts. A few months later, Colonel Kearny led his Army of the West into the Plaza of Santa Fe and claimed Santa Fe and New Mexico for the United States.

Changes came quickly: the first American newspaper in English and Spanish was founded, regular mail service from Missouri to New Mexico was established, a stagecoach crossed the plains once a month, and the volume and value of goods shipped on the Santa Fe Trail tripled. A new archbishop instigated the opening of a hospital, an orphanage and schools. Even the look of Santa Fe changed as it adopted white picket fences, gabled houses, flower gardens and walkways. New ordinances prohibited the camping of the wagon trains on the Plaza, butchers could no longer slaughter on the Plaza, nor drunken men sleep there. Santa Fe was becoming civilized.

Meanwhile, the Hispanic and the Indian population felt threatened as more and more Anglo-American settlers ignored Spanish land grants and their rights to their ancestral lands. There were increased attacks on settlers by Indians and attempts at insurrection by Hispanic New Mexicans. When, in 1880, the first engine steamed into Santa Fe, followed by demands for cattle and sheep, the Indian- and Spanish-Americans lost the lands that had been theirs for centuries to land speculators and cattle companies.

New Mexico became the 47th state on January 6, 1912. During the 1920's, New Mexico's heritage, its beautiful scenery and unusual colors attracted artists from all over the United States, who in turn gave the American public fascinating descriptions of the landscape, architecture and arts and crafts of the Southwest.

Today, Santa Fe with its opera, concerts, museums, galleries, special shows, dances and theaters is recognized as one of the nation's cultural meccas.

L'HISTOIRE DE SANTA FE.

L'été 1598, une longue caravane de charrettes, d'animaux de bât, de chevaux, de bétail, 129 soldats avec leurs familles et servants indiens, ainsi que huit Franciscains arrivèrent sur le haut du fleuve Rio Grande pour y construire une colonie espagnole permanente.

Les pionniers eurent de grandes difficultés à s'établir et, décimés par des révoltes indiennes et des désertions, abandonnèrent leur première colonie et recommencèrent au bord d'une petite rivière.

La Villa Real de Santa Fe (la Cité Royale de la Sainte Foi) fut établi sous l'ordre du roi d'Espagne, Philip III, comme capitale de la province du Nouveau Mexique par le gouverneur Don Pedro de Peralta, en 1610.

La vie dans la nouvelle cité n'était pas facile, mais petit à petit les colonistes s'adaptèrent au climat et à l'arridité du terrain, et abandonnant leurs rêves de trouver les fabuleuses "Cités d'Or", commencèrent à coloniser la nouvelle province espagnole. Chaque famille reçut assez de terrain pour une maison et un jardin, et 54 hectares de champs pour y cultiver de la vigne et des oliviers. En échange, les colonisateurs étaient obligés de vivre dans la cité pour dix ans, de cultiver leurs champs, de maintenir les fosses d'irrigation et d'être prêts à servir leur roi comme soldats. Au 17e siècle, la population de Santa Fe comptait 250 fermiers, artisans, commerçants, missionnaires et 750 servants indiens. Les petites maisons d'adobe des pionniers entouraient la Plaza fortifiée, tandis que les servants vivaient de l'autre côté de la rivière. La Plaza avec ses casas reales (l'administration) et son église était le centre civil et spirituel de la province.

Bien que le roi d'Espagne, le vice-roi du Mexique et les lois des Indes grantissaient la protection des indiens, ceux-ci souffrirent aux mains des Espagnols. Ils durent travailler pour les propriétaires fonciers et les missionnaires sans être payés, ne purent pas pratiquer leur religion ou vivre selon les traditions le leurs ancêtres, et durent donner des peaux, du maïs et des couvertures en tribut. En 1680, le ressentiment des indiens éclata dans la Révolte de Pueblo. Les Espagnols durent abandonner Santa Fe et le Nouveau-Mexique. Pendant douze ans, ils furent exilés à El Paso. En 1692, le nouveau gouverneur, Diego de Vargas, reprit la cité.

La vie de Santa Fe au 18e siècle ne changeait que peu. Les gens troquaient des piments, des moutons et d'autres produits contre des services, des marchandises et des terrains. Le gouverneur continuait ses disputes avec les Franciscains et le cabildo (gouvernement), les Santa Féans continuaient à se rejouir aux bals, aux fiestas et aux combats de coqs. Ils allaient à la Plaza voir des parades, des présentations de théâtre et des dances indiennes. Les meubles et les décorations des maisons étaient simples. On faisait la cuisine à feu ouvert ou dehors dans des "hornos", des fourneaux en forme de ruches.

Après la Révolte de Pueblo, la condition sociale des indiens s'améliora un peu. Bien que les gouverneurs, les propriétaires et les administrateurs des pueblos demandaient encore des tributs sous forme de produits agricoles et de travaux forcés, ils étaient libres de vivre selon leurs traditions et rituels religieux.

En 1821, un événement allait changer l'avenir de toutes les possessions espagnoles au nouvau monde. Le Mexique gagna son indépendance de l'Espagne. Petit à petit la vie au Nouveau-Mexique commença à changer. La nouvelle constitution mexicaine accorda la citoyenneté aux indiens, libéra le commerce, garantit la liberté d'expression et abolit les castes sociales instaurées par les Espagnols.

Encore en 1821, le marchand William Becknell partit de Franklin, Missouri, avec une caravane chargée d'articles de luxe. Il arriva au Nouveau-Mexique trois mois plus tard aux acclamations de tout Santa Fe. Dans les années suivantes la route à travers les plaines d'Amérique devint une route importante du commerce international. Bientôt le marché de Santa Fe fut saturé et les commerçants continuèrent avec leurs caravanes sur l'ancien Camino Real jusqu'à Chihuahua City au Mexique. Santa Fe devint le centre d'un commerce vivant. Quelques unes des caravanes avaient plus de 600 charrettes, avec 750 charretiers et guides, et amenaient des marchandises de plus d'un million de dollars. Du Mexique ils amenaient de l'argent en lingots, des fourrures et des toisons de moutons.

En 1846, le congrès américain déclara la guerre au Mexique pour régler la frontière entre le Texas et le Mexique, ainsi que le statut du Texas qu'il avait admis à l'Union en 1845. Quelques mois plus tard, le colonel Kearny et son Armée de l'Ouest, entrèrent dans la Plaza de Santa Fe en vainqueurs, et reclamèrent le Nouveau-Mexique pour les États-Unis.

La vie changea de nouveau. Un journal en anglais et espagnol informait les Santa Féans des événements politiques à Washington et à New York, un transport postal entre le Missouri et le Nouveau-Mexique les lia à l'est, et une fois par mois, la diligence amenait des visiteurs à travers la Prairie. La valeur des marchandises transportées par la route de Santa Fe se multiplia. Un nouvel archevêque vint de France et commença à construire un hôpital, un orphelinat et des écoles. Même la cité changea: des clôtures blanches, des maisons à pignons, des jardins de fleurs et des trottoirs longèrent les rues. Des ordonnances interdirent aux caravanes de camper sur la Plaza, aux bouchers d'y abattre les bestiaux et aux ivrognes d'y dormir. Santa Fe devint civilisée.

En attendant, dans la campagne, les indiens et les rancheros hispaniques durent se défendre contre les colonisateurs américains qui, ignorant leurs droits sur les terres, occupèrent des terrains qui avaient été les leurs depuis des centaines d'années. Quand en 1880, le chemin de fer joignit le Nouveau-Mexique à la côte atlantique de l'Amérique, ils perdirent leurs terrains aux spéculateurs et aux compagnies d'élévage.

Le 6 Janvier 1912, le Nouveau-Mexique devint le 47e état.

Pendant les années 1920, des artistes de tous les coins du monde arrivèrent au Nouveau-Mexique, attirés par son histoire, ses traditions, son paysage et ses couleurs. Ils fournirent au public des descriptions fascinantes du pays, des arts et métiers, et de l'architecture.

Aujourd'hui, Santa Fe avec son opéra, ses musées, ses ensembles de dance et de théâtre est une des centres culturels des États-Unis.

DIE GESCHICHTE DER STADT SANTA FE.

Im Sommer des Jahres 1598 kam eine lange, schwerfällige Karawane, bestehend aus Wagen, Lasttieren, Pferden, Schafen, Rindern, acht Franziskaner Missionären und 129 Siedlern sowie deren Familien und indianische Diener an den Oberlauf des Rio Grande, um die erste spanische Kolonie in Neu Mexico zu errichten.

Die ersten Siedlungen waren nicht erfolgreich und wurden schließlich aufgegeben. Die durch Hunger, Desertation und Indianerrevolten stark dezimierten Siedler beschlossen etwas südlicher am Ufer des Santa Fe Flusses neu zu beginnen.

1610 legte Don Pedro de Peralta, der zweite Gouverneur der Provinz, den Grundstein für "la Villa Real de Santa Fe" (die königliche Stadt des heiligen Glaubens) und ernannte sie auf Befehl Phillips III., König von Spanien, zur Hauptstadt von Nuevo Mejico.

Das Leben in der neuen Hauptstadt war schwierig, jedoch lernten die Siedler sich dem harten Land anzupassen und konzentrierten sich, nachdem sie endlich den Traum, die legendären Städte aus Gold zu finden, aufgegeben hatten, darauf, die neue Provinz zu kolonisieren. Jede Familie erhielt zwei Parzellen Land für ein Haus und einen Garten, zwei Felder für Wein- und Olivenanbau und zusätzlich 330 Hektar Land. Als Gegenleistung mußten sie sich verpflichten, zehn Jahre in Santa Fe zu leben, das Land zu bebauen, die Bewässerungskanäle in gutem Stand zu halten und bereit zu sein, ihrem Gouverneur als Soldaten ohne Bezahlung zur Verfügung zu stehen. Während des 17. Jahrhunderts zählte die Bevölkerung Santa Fes 250 Bauern, Handwerker, Händler, Missionäre und andere Grenzansiedler, außerdem lebten noch 750 Diener auf der anderen Seite des Flusses. Die Siedler wohnten in flachen Adobehäusern rund um die Plaza, die das geistige und weltliche Zentrum der Stadt war.

Obwohl die Verordnungen des spanischen Königs und des Vizekönigs von Mexiko, wie auch die Gesetze der Kolonien versuchten, die Indianer vor Ausnützungen durch die Gouverneure und Siedler zu schützen, litten die Indianer sehr unter der Herrschaft der Spanier. Sie mußten schwere Fronarbeiten leisten, durften ihre religiösen Zeremonien nicht ausüben und mußten übertriebene Tribute an Mais, Häuten und Decken an den Gouverneur und einige privilegierte Siedler entrichten. 1680 war die Geduld der Indianer am Ende und sie lehnten sich gegen diese Ausbeutung auf. Die Pueblo Revolte endete mit der Flucht der Spanier nach El Paso, wo sie 12 Jahre lang im Exil lebten.

Im Jahre 1692 eroberte Diego de Vargas, neuernannter Gouverneur von Neu Mexico, die Stadt zurück und begann Santa Fe wiederaufzubauen.

Das 18. Jahrhundert brachte nur wenige Veränderungen. Die Einwohner tauschten immer noch Paprikaschoten, Getreide, Erbsen, Schafe und andere Produkte gegen Dienstleistungen, Konsumgüter und sogar Land ein – Geld wurde erst gegen Ende des Jahrhunderts eingeführt. Der Gouverneur stritt sich weiterhin mit den geistlichen Brüdern und dem "Cabildo" (Regierung), während die Santa Feaner das Leben bei Tänzen, Festen und in Spielhallen genossen. Sie verwetteten ihr Geld bei Hahnenkämpfen, sahen sich Festzüge, Indianertänze oder dramatische Theatervorführungen über geschichtliche und biblische Themen in der Plaza an. Die Häuser waren einfach eingerichtet und geschmückt. Die Möbel und der Zierat wurden meistens in der Umgebung hergestellt. Die Mahlzeiten wurden entweder in grossen Töpfen im offenen Kamin oder in "Hornos" vor dem Hause gekocht und in Pueblos-Keramikwaren serviert.

Nach dem Pueblo Aufstand verbesserten sich die Lebensbedingungen der Indianer etwas, obwohl sie immer noch riesige Abgaben an den Gouverneur, die Landbesitzer und an die Verwalter der Pueblos bezahlen mußten, aber zumindest gab die Regierung den Versuch, sie in die spanische Gesellschaft einzugliedern, auf, und die Kirche ignorierte ihre religiösen Zeremonien und Bräuche.

1821 trat etwas ein, was die Zukunft aller spanischen Besitzungen in Amerika ändern sollte: Mexiko wurde eine unabhängige Republik. Die neue mexikanische Verfassung brachte Handels- und Redefreiheit, die Abschaffung des spanischen Kastensystems, volle Staatsbürgerrechte für die Indianer und direkte Besteuerung.

William Becknell, ein Händler in Franklin, Missouri, machte sich 1821 mit einer Anzahl von Packeseln, beladen mit Kurzwaren und Luxusgütern, auf den Weg. Seine mühsame Reise durch zum Teil feindliches Indianergebiet endete drei Monate später, als er unter großem Hurra der Bevölkerung in der Plaza von Santa Fe ankam. In den folgenden Jahren wurde der Santa Fe Trail zu einem häufig benützten Durchzugsweg. Allerdings war der Santa Fe Markt bald erschöpft, und die Händler mußten sich nach neuen Absatzmärkten umsehen. Innerhalb kürzester Zeit plagten sich die schwerfälligen Züge auf dem alten Camino Real (königlichen Weg) nach Chihuahua City. Santa Fe, wo die Händler ihre Abgaben leisten mußten, wurde das wohlhabende Zentrum eines lebhaften Handels in beiden Richtungen. Manche Karawanen bestanden aus 636 Wagen mit 750 Fuhrmännern und Viehtreibern und beförderten Güter im Werte von einer Million Dollar. Auf dem Rückweg nach Missouri waren die Wagen mit mexikanischen Silberbarren, Fellen, Häuten und Schafsfellen beladen.

1846 erklärte der amerikanische Kongreß Mexiko den Krieg, damit endlich die Grenzlinie zwischen Texas und Mexiko und der Status des 1845 in die Union aufgenommenen Staates Texas geklärt werde. Einige Monate später führte Oberst Kearny seine "Armee des Westens" im Siegeszug in die Plaza von Santa Fe.

Änderungen kamen schnell: eine english-spanische Zeitung informierte die Bevölkerung über die Vorkommnisse in Washington und New York, ein regelmässiger Postdienst verband Missouri mit dem neuen Gebiet, und einmal im Monat durchquerte die Postkutsche die Ebene von Kansas. Die Menge der Güter, die über den Santa Fe Trail kamen, vermehrte sich um ein Vielfaches. Ein neuer Erzbischof veranlaßte die Stadtväter, Kranken- und Waisenhäuser zu bauen und Schulen zu eröffnen. Sogar das Aussehen der Stadt veränderte sich. Weiße Gartenzäune, Giebelhäuser, Blumengärten und Stadtverordnungen, die das Campieren der Karawanen und das Schlachten von Tieren auf der Plaza verboten, kamen mit dem Bevölkerungszuzug aus dem Osten.

Die spanische und indianische Bevölkerung fühlte sich allerdings immer mehr bedroht, da die anglo-amerikanischen Behörden und Siedler ihre spanischen und indianischen Landbesitzrechte nicht anerkannten. Indianerangriffe auf Siedler und Aufstände nahmen zu. Als 1880 die erste Lokomotive in Santa Fe einfuhr, verloren die Indianer und Spanish Mexikaner ihren Kampf um ihren Besitz endgültig an landgierige Spekulanten und Viehzüchter.

Am 6. Januar 1912 wurde Neu Mexiko als der 47. Staat in die Vereinigten Staaten aufgenommen.

Während der zwanziger Jahre kamen viele Künstler, angezogen von Neu Mexikos Geschichte und Bräuchen, seiner schönen Landschaft und ungewöhnlichen Farbtönen nach Santa Fe und Taos. Diese Maler und Schriftsteller vermittelten den Amerikanern betörende Bilder und Beschreibungen von dem, was sie in dem bisher unbekannten Südwesten sahen.

Santa Fe gehört heute mit seinen Opernfestspielen, seinen Konzerten, Kunstgalerien, Theater- und Tanzvorführungen und Museen zu den kulturellen Zentren der Vereinigten Staaten.

Events Calendar:

Pueblo Fiestas and Dances are held throughout the year. For information call, Tourist Division, Eight Northern Pueblos, (505) 852-4265.

Rodeo de Santa Fe, July. Tel.: (505) 982-4659

Spanish Market, last weekend in July. Tel.: (505) 983-4038

La Fiesta de Santa Fe, weekend after Labor Day. Tel.: (505) 988-7575

Santa Fe Opera, July and August. Tel.: (505) 982-3855

Indian Market, August. Tel.: (505) 983-5220

Arts and Crafts Fairs, throughout the year. Tel.: (505) 984-6760

Santa Fe Festivals of the Arts. Tel.: (505) 988-3924

Festivals at Rancho de las Golondrinas. Tel.: (505) 471-2261

Horse Racing at Downs at Santa Fe on Wednesdays, Fridays, Saturdays, Sundays and holidays from the middle of June through Labor Day. Tel.: (505) 471-3311

Winter Fiesta, February. Tel.: (505) 983-5615

Acknowledgements:
My special thanks are due to:

Mr. and Mrs. Jean-Michel Bock
Mrs. Elisabeth Torggler Schafer
El Rancho de las Golondrinas
Guadalupe Historic Foundation
Kit Carson Historic Museums
Millicent Rogers Museum
Pecos National Monument
The Bishop's Lodge Resort

Photographs courtesy of

Museum of New Mexico, pages 3 and 28,
  photo by Michel Monteaux
Museum of New Mexico, Photo Archives #11330, page 8
  and #87450, page 30
Museum of Indian Arts and Culture/Laboratory of
  Anthropology #36593, page 26, Zuni Polychrome Jar,
  photo by Douglas Kahn
Wheelwright Museum of the American Indian, page 27,
  photo by Bruce Hucko
The Santa Fe Children's Museum, page 29,
  photo by Richard A. Abeles
The Santa Fe Opera, page 33, photo by Murrae Haynes
New Mexico Economic and Tourism Department, pages 34,
  45, 54, photos by Mark Nohl

The author gratefully acknowledges the invaluable assistance of Gabriele Lutz in producing 23 of the photographs.

Museum of Fine Arts, 107 West Palace Ave., built in 1917, the first building in the Spanish-Pueblo Revival style, was modeled after the 1915 New Mexico State Exposition Building at the San Diego Exposition, which helped promote the rich architectural heritage of the Southwest. The Spanish Colonial-style furniture was designed for the museum.

Museum of Fine Arts. Santa Fe and Taos have attracted writers, poets, musicians, photographers and sculptors since the 1880's, however, it was the painters of the 1920's and 30's who were the most influential on the American art scene with their brilliant light and unusual subjects. The "Art in New Mexico: The Early Years" exhibit is on the second floor.

Museum of Fine Art, "Red Hills and Pedernal," by Georgia O'Keeffe, 1936. The most famous of all the painters drawn to northern New Mexico, O'Keeffe lived for many years in nearby Abiquiu.

Palace of the Governors, Plaza, has been in continuous use since 1610. The original structure, called "Casas Reales" (Royal Houses), consisted of workrooms, stables, storage rooms, defense towers, a chapel, a garrison and living quarters of the governor. In 1680, during the Pueblo Revolt, about 1,000 Spaniards, their servants and livestock gathered within Casas Reales. When the Spaniards fled the city, the Indians remodeled the palace into a multistoried pueblo. Today it houses the History Museum.

Indian artists spread their handmade crafts under the "portal" of the Palace of the Governors.

Around the Plaza.

Sena Plaza, Palace Avenue. In the 19th century, this courtyard was the scene of grand Spanish hospitality. The hacienda for the big Sena family, had 33 rooms and a ballroom big enough to hold the legislative assembly when the capitol burned in 1892.

Photo (ca 1868) of the old "parroquia" (parish church) and East San Francisco Street. Between 1869 and 1886, the new cathedral was built around the old parish church, a simple adobe structure started in 1714, parts of which can still be seen in the Chapel of our Lady of the Rosary.

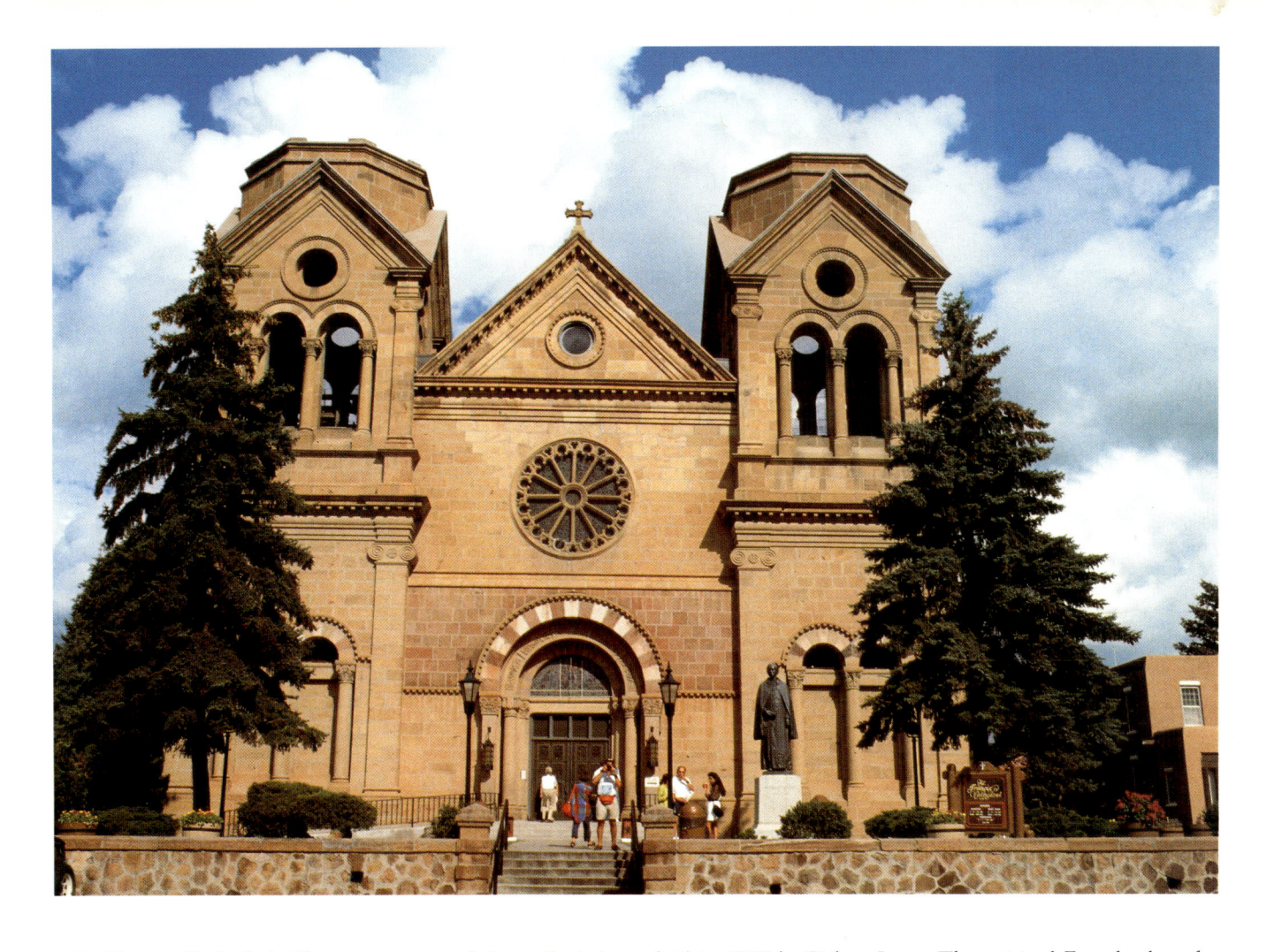

St. Francis Cathedral. The cornerstone of the cathedral was laid in 1869 by Bishop Lamy. The original French plans for the cathedral called for steeples to rise 160 feet from the two towers, they were never built.

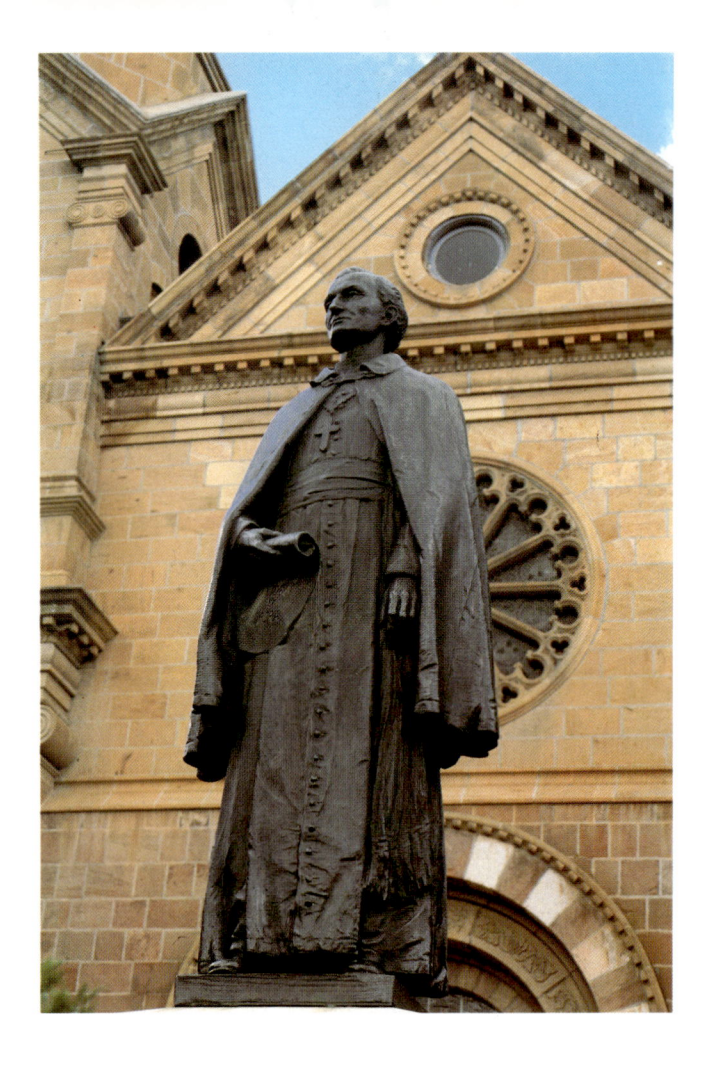

Bishop Lamy, arrived in Santa Fe in 1851 at the height of New Mexico's wild frontier period, during which the influence of the catholic church declined. Bishop Lamy energetically brought his flock back into the church, established schools, orphanages and hospitals, and gradually instilled a sense of refinement into Santa Fe life. Willa Cather described Lamy's life in Santa Fe in "Death Comes For The Archbishop."

Details from the Cathedral. The sixteen door panels depict the history of Santa Fe. Here: the flight of Santa Feans with their "Conquistadora to El Paso del Norte" in 1680. This carved stone angel reminds us of French churches. Lamy employed stonecutters from Italy and France, however the stone came from nearby quarries.

La Coquistadora, was carved in Mexico and brought to Santa Fe in 1625. She was originally known as Our Lady of the Assumption but was renamed "La Conquistadora" (Our Lady of the Conquest) after she accompanied the Spanish into exile from 1680 - 1692 and returned with Diego de Vargas when he reconquered the territory.

Institute of American Indian Arts Museum, Cathedral Place. This museum features exhibitions of contemporary Native American art.

Loretto Chapel, 219 Old Santa Fe Trail. The Sisters of Loretto who had arrived in Santa Fe at the request of Bishop Lamy had this Gothic chapel built in the 1870s. They operated a school for girls at the site of the present Inn at Loretto.

Legend has it that upon completion of the chapel the sisters discovered that the architect had forgotten to include in his plans a stairway to the choir loft and that a conventional stairway would not fit. The sisters were distressed and prayed to St. Joseph, the patron saint of carpenters, for help. Before long a carpenter appeared and constructed this circular staircase without a center support or nails. When the mysterious carpenter had finished his masterpiece he disappeared without any pay.

Inn at Loretto.

Barrio del Analco is perhaps the oldest residential neighborhood in the nation. The Spanish who lived on the north side of the river decreed that their Indian allies and servants had to reside on the south side. The Indians built their houses upon the ruins of an old pueblo. Noteworthy are the Gregorio Crespin House (132 E. De Vargas, not shown) and the "Oldest House in the USA" (215 E. De Vargas) which is a good example of adobe construction, the walls are made of poured mud.

San Miguel Chapel, Old Santa Fe Trail/East De Vargas. This chapel was originally built around 1610 by Mexican Indian servants who lived on the south bank of the Santa Fe River. San Miguel was heavily damaged during the Pueblo Revolt, and was rebuilt in 1710. The altar screens were painted in Mexico in 1798, the central statue of St. Michael dates from the seventeenth century.

Santuario de Guadaloupe, 100 Guadaloupe Street. This adobe church was built between 1776 and 1795 near the end of the Camino Real, a colonial trade route connecting Mexico City with the northern provinces. The oil-on canvas Spanish barock altar painting was created in Mexico City in 1783 by Jose de Alzibar. It was brought in pieces on mule back up the Camino Real and assembled here. The Santa Fe Desert Chorale performs in the Santuario.

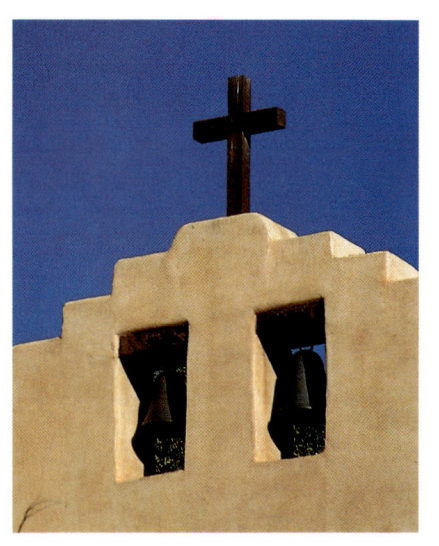

Architectural styles: Rosario Chapel, First Presbyterian Church, Bishop's Chapel, detail Museum of Art (clockwise).

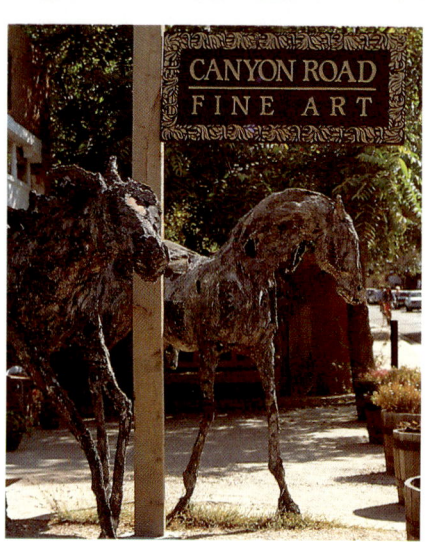

Canyon Road. The Pueblo Indians established it as a trail over the Sangre de Christo Mountains to Pecos Pueblo. The Spanish conquistadores called the route "El Camino Real de Cañon" (The Royal Road of the Canyon). Today, Canyon Road houses more than 80 galleries, artists' studios, boutiques, specialty stores, restaurants and historic houses.

Christo Rey Church, Canyon Road. Built with more than 180,000 adobe bricks in 1940 to commemorate Coronado's expedition into New Mexico in 1540. Architect John Gaw Meem designed it in classical Spanish mission style.

Reredos (altar screens) in Christo Rey Church. These ornately carved stone altar screens were carved around 1760 by Mexican stone carvers for the military chapel of "La Castrense," which stood on the south side of the Plaza.

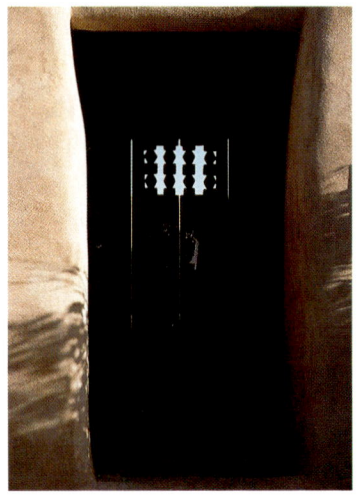

Doors on Camino del Monte Sol.

24

25

Museum of Indian Arts & Culture, 710 Camino Lejo. This relatively new museum concentrates on Pueblo, Navajo and Apache Indian peoples of the Southwest. In addition to exhibitions of artifacts from the Laboratory of Anthropology's collection, it presents demonstrations and workshops by Indian basket makers, potters, jewelers and weavers. Shown on this picture is a Zuni jar, ca. 1870, featuring "rainbird" motifs.

Wheelwright Museum, 704 Camino Lejo, was originally built by Mary Cabot Wheelwright to house her extensive records of Navajo ceremonies, myths, songs, sandpaintings, as well as her collection of Navajo basketry, jewelry and textiles. The collection has since expanded to include examples of the craft arts of other Southwestern Indian groups. The museum is in the shape of a traditional Navajo dwelling, the hogan. Shown on this page are Navajo silver and turquoise jewelry pieces.

Museum of International Folk Art, 706 Camino Lejo. This museum centers around two permanent exhibits: the Girard collection, a richly varied display of about 10,000 pieces representing the folk art of over 100 countries; and the Hispanic Heritage Wing, an exhibition interpreting the importance of family and faith to the New Mexican Hispanic culture.

Children's Museum of Santa Fe, 1050 Old Pecos Trail. Hands-on activities challenge children and adults alike to play, question and discover.

Caravan on the Santa Fe Trail, 1830. When New Mexico became part of Mexico in 1821, American traders, prohibited by Spanish law to sell their wares in the province, realized they could make fortunes by bringing luxury items from Franklin, MO, to the capital of the New Mexico district. The arrival of the wagon trains from the plains was a spectacle no Santa Fean would have missed, for the "Americanos" also brought news and foreign ideas to the isolated people of the Southwest.

With the opening of the West a new breed of adventurers crossed the plains and entered the mountains to hunt beavers. These trappers or mountain men learned the crafts of the wilderness and knew the unchartered terrain of the prairies and mountains almost as well as the Indians.

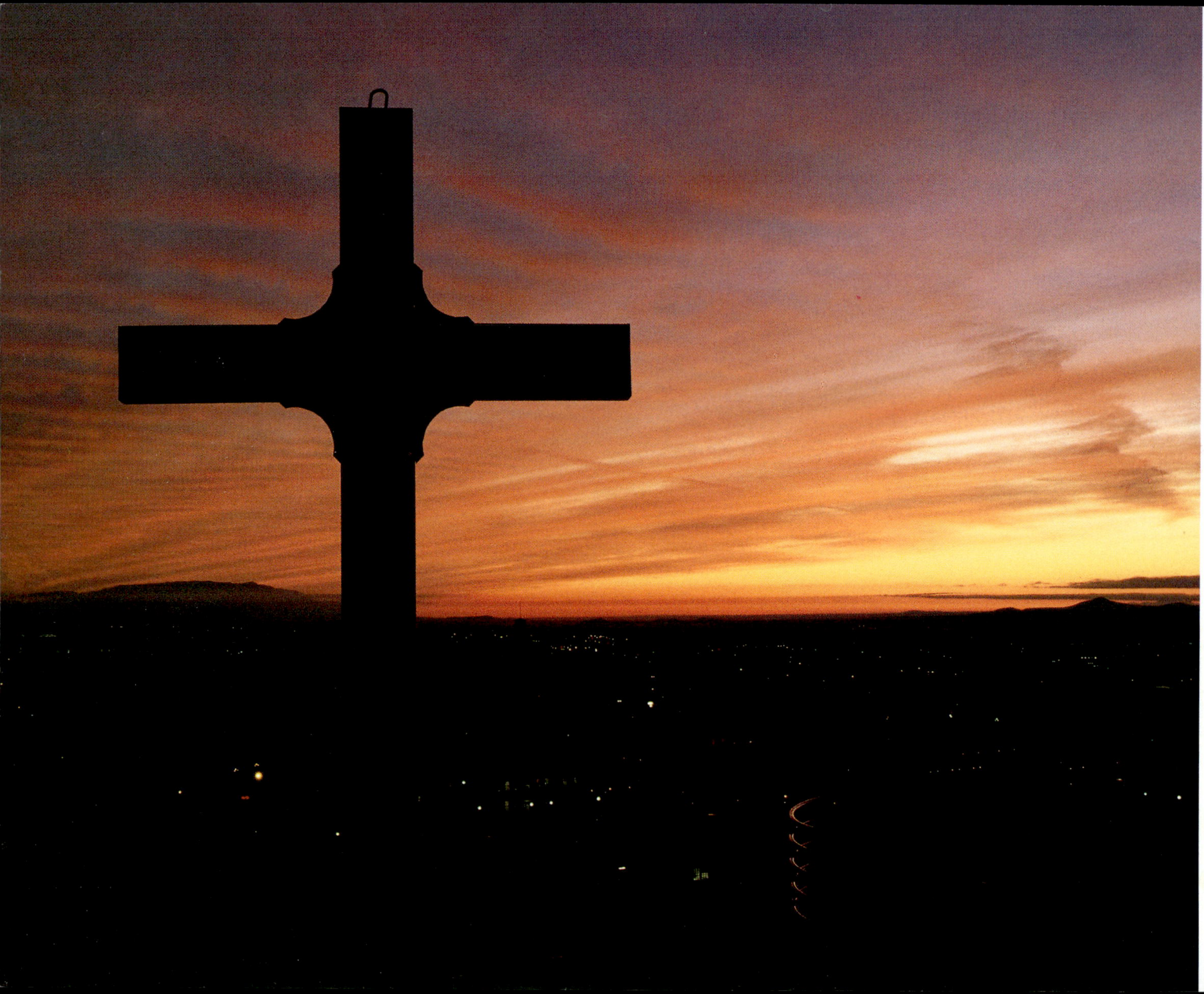

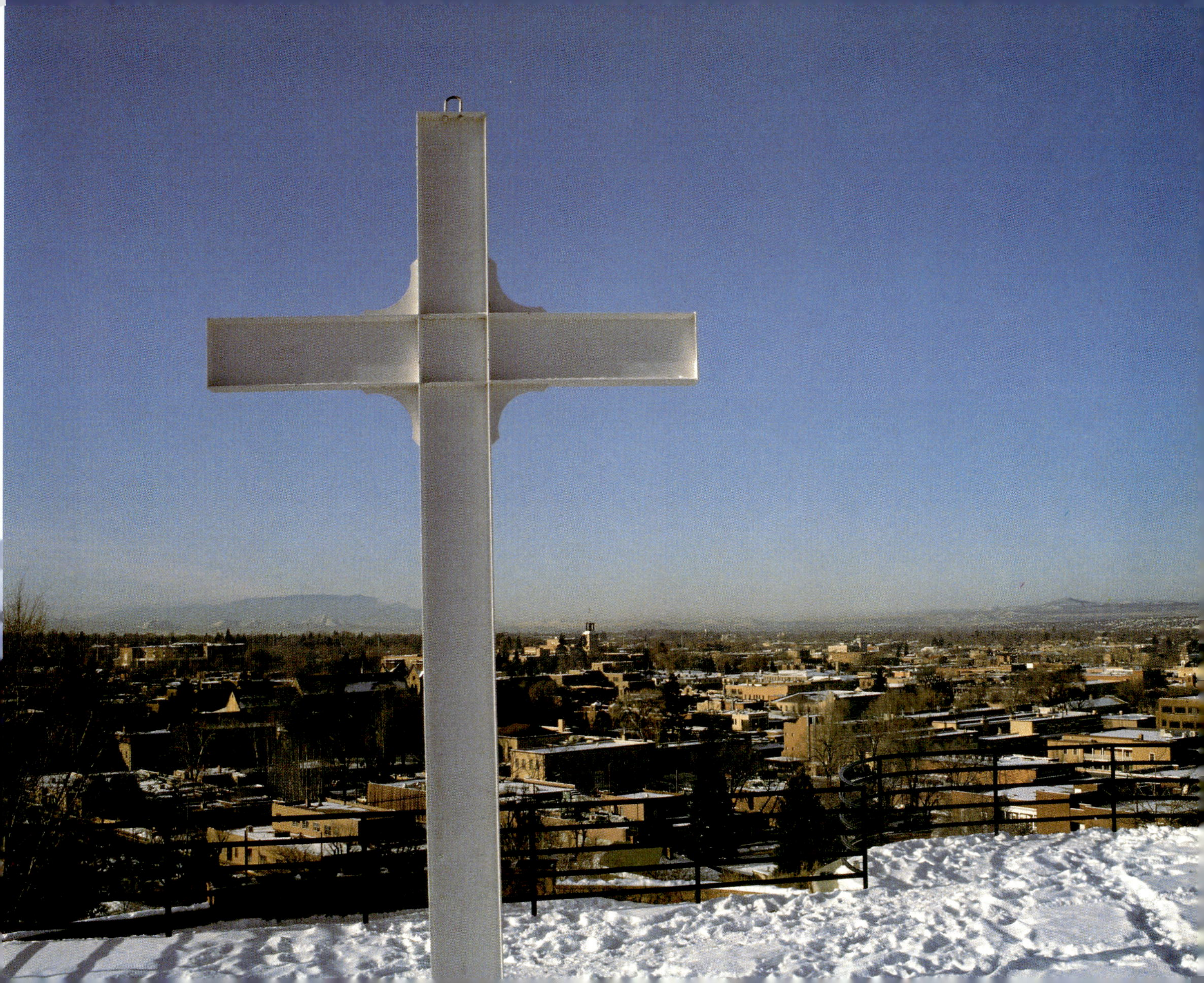

Fiesta de Santa Fe. The first Fiesta was celebrated in 1712, when it was decreed that De Vargas' reconquest of Santa Fe in 1692 was to be commemorated with an annual fiesta. This celebration blends a mixture of cultures - from De Vargas' "entrada" (historical pageant) to "desfile de las Fiestas" (parade); from the solemn Mass to the burning of "Zozobra" which marks the end of gloom and the beginning of fun.

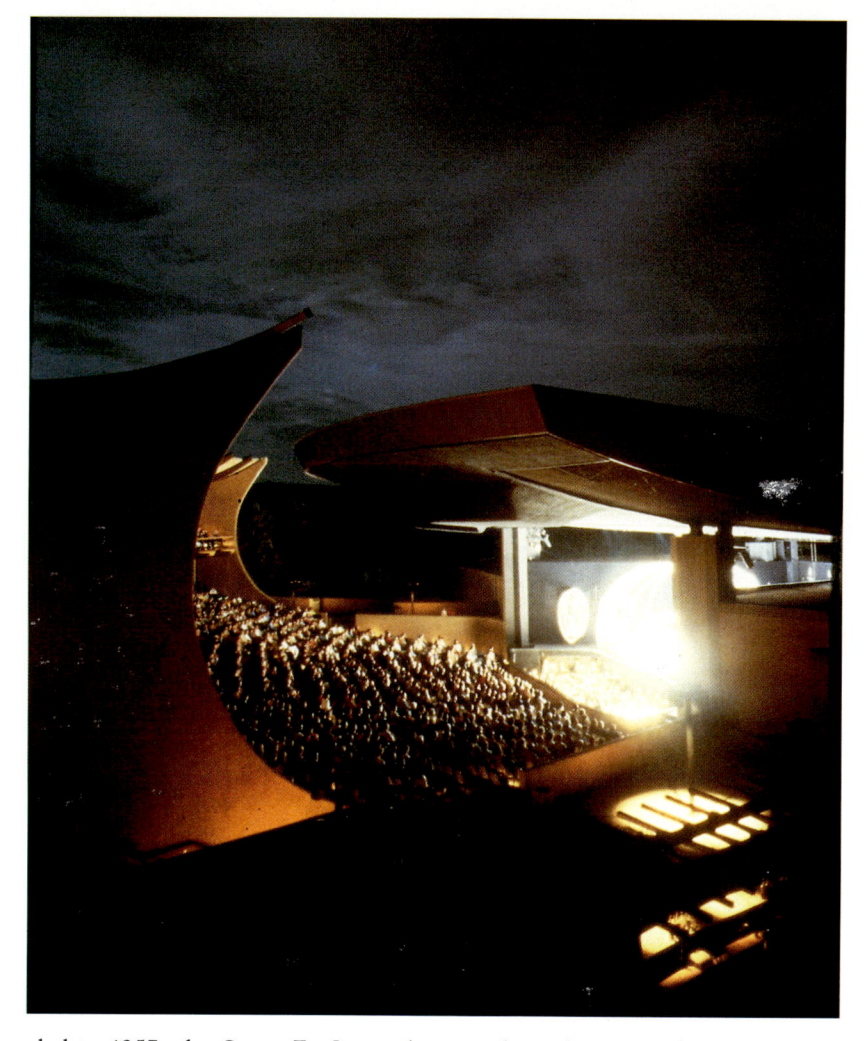

Santa Fe Opera. Founded in 1957, the Santa Fe Opera draws acclaimed singers, directors, conductors and designers - as well as huge crowds during its eight-week season.

El Rancho de las Golondrinas, La Cienega. The Ranch of the Swallows was a hacienda and the last stopping place for the caravans and travelers on the Camino Real (The Royal Road) from Mexico City. A living museum of the region's Spanish colonial heritage, this working ranch includes 18th and 19th century houses and their outbuildings, a blacksmith shop, several water mills, a winery and vineyards. Also on the grounds are re-creations of a Spanish village, a meeting house and a cemetery.

The main buildings of El Rancho de las Golondrinas were built around a central "placita," with a defensive tower on one side of the fortress-like compound. In case of an attack by hostile Indians the farm animals and wagons were hastily driven into the square and the gates closed.

The Morada de la Conquistadora, El Rancho de las Golondrinas. This meeting house of the Brotherhood of Los Penitentes is a reconstruction of the "morada" at Abiquiu. The Penitentes were a lay brotherhood who devoted themselves to the commemoration of the suffering and death of Jesus Christ and to penitential practices. Their folk religion spread rapidly in Northern New Mexico towards the end of the eighteenth century.

Santuario de Chimayo, Chimayo. This small chapel, which is sometimes called the Lourdes of the Southwest, is one of the most revered places in New Mexico. The ground on which the chapel is built is reputed to have miraculous healing powers. The facade and the religious folk art inside are typical of the Spanish frontier churches of the early nineteenth century. Chimayo is also a center for Spanish weaving.

San Jose de Gracias Chapel in Las Trampas. The chapel is one of the most beautiful Spanish colonial churches in the state. Las Trampas was founded by 12 families from Santa Fe in 1751.

St. Francis Church in Ranchos de Taos, built in 1776. The massive adobe walls and buttresses of this small mission church have been the subject of countless photographs and paintings. Ansel Adams called it "One of the great architectural monuments in America." Ranchos de Taos was settled by the Spanish in 1716.

Hyde Memorial Park. Hyde Park Road, which ends at the Santa Fe Ski Basin, climbs from seven thousand feet to 10,260 feet.

Several trails start along Hyde Park Road, like the Aspen Vista Trail which leads through aspen, fir and spruce forests to Tesuque Peak (12,040 feet).

Shidoni Sculpture Garden, Tesuque. Eight acres of sculpture gardens and two galleries show sculptures from artists from all over the country.

Indian Ceremonials and Dances. Shown here clockwise: Olla Maidens in the Gallup Tribal Ceremonial, Deer Dance at San Ildefonso, and a young dancer at San Juan Pueblo.

45

Pecos National Monument. Ruins of this ancient pueblo go back to the 1400's, when Pecos was a thriving pueblo of 2,000 people. Its quadrangle, built around a central plaza, was four to five stories high, included up to 660 rooms and more than 20 ceremonial kivas. At the time of Coronado's arrival the village was an important trading center between the Plains Indians to the East and the Pueblo Indians to the West. Shown here is a diorama of the North Pueblo displayed in the museum.

Pecos National Monument. The Franciscan friars arrived in the 1600's bringing Christianity, European farming methods, apples, apricots, wheat, cattle and many other things. In return the Indians introduced the Spaniards to their herbal medicine and methods of irrigation, and to such crops as corn, beans and squash. A mission church was erected in 1620 only to be destroyed in the revolt of 1680. The massive walls of the second church served as a landmark to travelers on the Santa Fe Trail.

Los Cerrillos. Before the arrival of the Spanish the mineral-rich area around Los Cerrillos produced turquoise which was traded as far as the Valley of Mexico. The town hit its peak in the late 1800's, when gold, silver, lead and zinc were mined in great quantities. It supported 21 saloons then. Los Cerrillos (Little Hills) has been the scene of several western films. Shown here is the "Cerrillos Turquoise Mining Museum."

Madrid, once a thriving coal mining town, was founded in the mid-1800's. It was purchased fifty years later by the Albuquerque and Cerrillos Coal Co. which operated the mines till 1959 when everything was shut down and Madrid became a ghost town. Since then the town has started to come to life again as an artists' colony.

The AT & SF (Atchison, Topeka & Santa Fe Railroad) engine, at the Old Coal Mining Museum in Madrid. In 1880, the first engine steamed into Santa Fe on a spur from the main line which passed through nearby Lamy on its way to Albuquerque. The railroad soon replaced the mule-drawn wagons of the Santa Fe Trail.

Church in Golden. Golden was the site of the first gold rush west of the Mississippi in 1825.

Sandia Crest. The 10,678 feet high summit of the Sandia Mountains offers sweeping views in all directions. Several hiking trails lead through aspen glades and across flowering meadows. The Sandia (Watermelon) Mountains were named because of the pink glow that covers the mountain tops at sunset.

Albuquerque was founded in 1706 in honor of the tenth Duke of Alburquerque (the "r" was subsequently dropped). From the beginning, Albuquerque was a trade and transportation center. The church, San Felipe de Neri, in the center of Old Town, still rests on its thick original walls.

The Albuquerque International Balloon Fiesta features 600 hot air balloons during nine days in October.

Impressions of New Mexico.

Bandelier National Monument, Frijoles Canyon. Inhabited by the Anasazi (the Ancient Ones) more than 600 years ago. They were farming people who grew their squash, beans and corn in the rich soil of the canyon floor and on the mesatops. They built multistoried, apartment-like structures around a central plaza and along the walls of the canyon, and carved dwellings into the porous cliffs.

As many as 550 people lived at one time in Frijoles Canyon. Nobody knows for sure why the Anasazi left their cliff dwellings and settled along the Rio Grande, but when the Spanish arrived in the late 1500's the stone rooms in Frijoles Canyon were deserted.

Martinez Hacienda, Ranchitos Road, Taos. This fortress-like hacienda was built around two placitas by Don Antonio Severino Martinez, around 1804. Don Antonio, a trader and owner of caravans in the profitable Chihuahua trade, was also "Alcalde" of Taos. His eldest son, Antonio Jose, became a priest and the spiritual and social leader of the Northern Rio Grande area.

Kit Carson House & Museum, East Kit Carson Road, Taos. Kit Carson came to New Mexico with a caravan commanded by Charles Brent, who later became the first American Governor of New Mexico. In 1843, the famous scout purchased this home as a wedding gift for his bride, Josefa Jamarillo. Three of the rooms are furnished as they might have been when Kit Carson and his family lived there. The museum offers exhibits about Carson and the Mountain Man Period.

Taos Pueblo is the northernmost of the 19 pueblos still in existence in New Mexico. The Tribe is descended from Anasazi Indian culture which flourished in the Four Corners Area of the Southwest from A.D. 100 to A.D. 1200. The Anasazi migration into the Taos area occurred as early as A.D. 900. When Coronado and his men saw Taos in 1540, they believed they had discovered one of the lost cities of gold. Virtually unchanged in appearance the north building has been lived in since about 1450.

Church in Taos Pueblo.

Taos Pueblo. The mountain creek that runs between the North and South Houses flows from sacred Blue Lake, high in the surrounding mountains. In 1970, President Nixon signed the bill returning title of the Blue Lake area to the Pueblo into law, thus ending the Pueblo's 60-year fight for return of its sacred lands, and marking the beginning of a new direction in Indian affairs.

Millicent Rogers Museum, off NM 522, Taos. The museum's original collection consists of southwestern native American jewelry, textiles, baskets, pottery and paintings assembled during the 1940's by Millicent Rogers. In recent years religious and secular artifacts of Hispanic New Mexico have been added, as well as the most extensive collection of Maria Martinez pottery anywhere. The sculpture on this page is by R.C. Gorman, a Navajo artist. It is located in the interior patio of the museum.

Rio Grande Gorge, US 64. A huge split in the earth's crust has resulted in the Rio Grande rift basin which filled with thousands of feet of alluvium from bordering mountains and lava flows from deep within the earth. The Rio Grande Gorge is about 650 feet deep.

サンタフェ ー 過去と現在

1598年の夏、幌馬車や荷物を積んだ牛馬、農耕馬、畜牛、羊、ヤギなどの長い行列が、ニューメキシコのリオグランデ川上流に到着した。ニューメキシコ初の恒久植民地開拓を目指すこの一行は、スペイン人兵士129名とその家族、メキシコ・インディアンの奴隷、そしてフランシスコ会修道士8名を含む移民たちであった。

しかし最初に開拓された二つの植民地は、飢餓、脱走、プエブロ族インディアンの反乱などで多くの移民を失ったために放棄され、新たな出発を期してサンタフェ川沿いに新植民地が建設された。

1610年、この植民地の第二代総督ドン・ペドロ・デ・ペラルタが、スペイン国王フィリップ三世の命を受けて、「ヌエボ・メヒコ(ニューメキシコ)」の首都ラ・ビラ・レアル・デ・サンタフェ(「聖なる信仰の勅認都市」)を設立した。

新たに築いた植民地での生活も、厳しく危険に満ちたものであった。しかし移民たちは徐々に環境に適応し、当初の目標であった伝説の「黄金都市」発見の夢をあきらめてサンタフェに根を下ろし、植民地建設に専念した。移民たちには、一家族につき住宅・庭園用に土地二区画、野菜畑用に隣接する土地二区画、葡萄畑・オリーブ畑用に二区画、さらに約133エーカー(54ヘクタール)の土地が支給された。土地及び用水権と引き替えに、彼らには、10年間継続してサンタフェに居住し、自分の土地に作物を栽培して、灌漑用溝の維持に協力し、必要時には無給で兵役に就く義務があった。17世紀初頭を通じて、サンタフェ植民地の人口は、農民・職人・商人・宣教師ら開拓者約250人、インディアン奴隷約750人を維持していた。移民たちは、塀に囲まれた広場の外のアドビ煉瓦造りの平屋に住み、インディアン奴隷の居住区は、サンタフェ川を隔てた別地区にあった。広場には一端に「カサス・レアレス(政庁舎)」、もう一端にアドビ造りの教会があり、首都サンタフェにおける市民活動と宗教活動の中心となっていた。

スペイン国王やメキシコの太守、さらにアメリカ植民地法も、明らかに総督以下植民者によるインディアンの虐待を防止する方針を立てていたが、実際にはスペイン人の統治下でプエブロ・インディアンたちは過酷な生活を強いられていた。彼らは、移民や宣教師に、無給あるいは無給同然の待遇で使われ、独自の宗教・生活慣習の実践を禁止された上、総督や、スペインでの軍務の報酬としてインディアン統治権を受託された移民らに、トウモロコシ、獣皮、毛布などの年貢を納めなければならなかった。1680年には、抑圧されたインディアンの怒りが爆発して「プエブロ族の反乱」が発生。スペイン人移民たちはサンタフェ及びニューメキシコからエルパソへ脱出し、以後12年間エルパソで暮らした。

1692年、ニューメキシコ植民地の新総督に任命されたディエゴ・デ・バルガスがサンタフェを奪還し、翌年には移民たちもサンタフェに戻って町の再建を始めた。

18世紀のサンタフェは、それまでとあまり変わらない植民生活が続いた。各種サービス・商品・土地の購入の支払いは、トウガラシ、トウモロコシ、豆、羊などの産物や動物による物々交換で行われた。通貨の使用が始まるのは18世紀末である。総督と修道士・政庁との争いが絶えず、一方で住民たちは、お祭り、舞踏会、賭博などを楽しんでいた。闘鶏、パレード、広場で行われるインディアンの踊り、歴史や聖書をテーマにした劇などが住民の娯楽となっていた。住宅のインテリアや家具は質素で、地元で作られたものが多かった。当時の食事は、重い大鍋を使って暖炉で煮炊きされるか、屋外にあるホルノスという蜂の巣の形をしたアドビ製の炉で調理された。食器には、プエブロ・インディアンの作った陶器を使用した。

プエブロ族の反乱後、インディアンの生活は多少改善されたが、総督、インディアン監督官、大地主らは、相変わらずインディアンたちから産物・労働による料金・罰金を取り立てていた。しかし植民地政府は、少なくともインディアンをスペイン人社会に同化させようとする努力は放棄し、教会もインディアンたちが行なう非キリスト教の儀式を見逃すようになった。

1821年、メキシコがスペインから独立した。これはアメリカにおけるスペイン領地の将来を大きく変える重大な出来事だった。ニューメキシコの生活も徐々に変わり始めた。メキシコの新憲法は、インディアンに市民権を与えるとともに、貿易の自由と言論の自

由を保証し、スペイン人種の純血度に基づく古くからのスペインの階級制度を廃止した。またニューメキシコの住民が 200年以上にわたって回避してきた直接税の制度も、この新憲法で実施された。

同じく1821年、ミズーリ州フランクリンの商人ウィリアム・ベックネルが、織物などを満載したロバを連れ、インディアンや猟師が踏みならした小道を通って、3カ月をかけてサンタフェにやってきた。サンタフェの住民は、広場に集まって大歓声でベックネルを迎え、待ちかねたように商品を買った。以後ニューメキシコへの道は重要な国際貿易路となったが、ほどなくサンタフェの市場は飽和状態となり、旧道カミノ・レアルを通ってメキシコのチワワ・シティへ向かう商人も増え出した。貨物を運ぶ商人は皆サンタフェの税関で関税を支払わなければならなかったため、サンタフェの町は、ミズーリとメキシコを往復する商人たちの集まる商業の中心地として栄えた。これらのキャラバンの中には、荷馬車 636台、御者及び牛追人 750名、輸送商品総額 100万ドルという大規模なものもあった。メキシコからミズーリへ帰るキャラバンは、メキシコ産の銀塊・毛皮・毛布・羊毛を満載していた。

1846年、米国議会はメキシコに対して宣戦を布告した。長年にわたって論争の種となっていたテキサスとメキシコの境界問題に決着をつけるためである。米国は1845年にテキサスを合衆国に併合したが、メキシコは依然としてテキサスを自国の一部と主張していた。数カ月後、カーニー大佐率いる西部軍がサンタフェの広場に攻め入り、サンタフェ及びニューメキシコをアメリカ合衆国領地とした。

メキシコ戦争後、サンタフェは急速に変化した。その一環として、初めてアメリカ人による英語とスペイン語の新聞が発行された。またミズーリ州とニューメキシコの間に定期郵便が開始され、月に一度は駅馬車が往復するようになった。サンタフェへの道を輸送される商品は、量・価格ともにそれまでの三倍に増えた。新任の大司教の指導で、病院・孤児院・学校が設立された。白塗りの柵、切妻の付いた家、花壇のある庭、歩道などが作られて、サンタフェの町の外観にも変化が現れた。新しい条例ができて、広場で幌馬車隊が野営すること、広場で屠殺を行うこと、また酔払って広場で寝ることが禁止された。サンタフェの文明化が始まったのである。

一方、スペイン人とインディアンたちは、スペイン国王から譲与された土地、あるいは先祖代々の土地に、英国系アメリカ人移民が我が物顔に入り込んでくることに不安をつのらせ、インディアンによる移民襲撃やニューメキシコのスペイン人による暴動計画なども増えていった。1880年、サンタフェに蒸気鉄道が初めて開通し、牛や羊の需要が急増すると、土地投機家や畜産業者がやって来て、インディアンやスペイン人移民は、何百年来の所有地を取り上げられてしまった。

ニューメキシコは、1912年1月6日、アメリカ合衆国の第47番目の州となった。1920年代には、ニューメキシコの歴史、美しい風土、そして他では見られない珍しい自然の色彩を求めてアメリカ全土から芸術家たちが集まってきた。彼らは、ニューメキシコの地形や建築、アメリカ南西部の美術工芸品の魅力を全米の大衆に知らせる役割を果たした。こうして芸術家や人類学者がスペイン人やプエブロ・インディアンの慣習・伝統の保存を呼びかけたこと、また観光客がプエブロ族の工芸品や踊りなどに興味を示し始めたことがきっかけとなって、スペイン人及びプエブロ族の伝統工芸や慣習が復活した。

今日のサンタフェは、オペラ、コンサート、画廊、博物館、展覧会、舞踏、劇場など、芸術の場に恵まれ、アメリカでも有数の文化都市として知られている。

Index — Santa Fe

LEGEND: ☗ Interesting and fun for children of all ages.

♿ Access for handicapped people.

♿ Partial access and/or with assistance.

All distances measured from Plaza unless otherwise stated.

Tour #1: DOWNTOWN

Page
1-3   Museum of Fine Arts ♿
Museum of New Mexico
107 West Palace Avenue
Tel.: (505) 827-4455
Hours: Daily 10-5 (Closed Jan. & Feb.)
Yes, 2-day pass to all museums (Palace of the Governors, Museum of Indian Arts & Culture, Museum of International Folk Art) available

4, 5   Palace of the Governors ♿
Museum of New Mexico
The Plaza
Tel.: (505) 827-6483
Hours: Daily 10-5 (Closed Jan. & Feb.)
Admission: Yes, 2-day pass to all museums (Museum of Fine Arts, Museum of Indian Arts & Culture, Museum of International Folk Art) available

9-12   San Francis Cathedral ♿
Cathedral Place
Tel.: (505) 982-5619
Hours: dawn - dusk
Admission: Free

Page
13   Institute of the American Indian Arts Museum ♿
Cathedral Place
Tel.: (505) 988-6603
Hours: Daily 10-6
Admission: Yes

14, 15   Loretto Chapel ♿
219 Old Santa Fe Trail
Tel.: (505) 984-7971
Hours: Daily 9-4:30
Admission: Donation

18   San Miguel Chapel
Old Santa Fe Trail and East De Vargas Street
Tel.: (505) 983-3970
Hours: Mon.-Sat. 9-4:30; Sun. 1-4:30
Admission: Free

19   Santuario de Guadalupe
100 Guadalupe Street
Tel.: (505) 988-2027
Hours: Mon.-Sat. 9-4, Sun. 12-4,
(Closed weekends Nov. - Apr.)
Admission: Donation

Tour #2: CANYON ROAD

Canyon Road is 1.1 miles long. From Camino del Monte Sol it is approximately 0.5 miles to:

Page
22, 23   Christo Rey Church
Upper Canyon Road and Alameda
Tel.: (505) 983-8528
Hours: Daily 7-7
Admission: Free

You can continue to tour #3, "Museums." Turn right on Camino del Monte Sol (approximately 0.9 mi.) turn right into Santa Fe Trail (0.1 mi.), left on Camino Lejo.

Tour #3: MUSEUMS

Take Old Santa Fe Trail south (0.7 miles), at fork with Old Pecos Trail turn left, go 0.8 miles, turn right into Camino Lejo.

Page
26   Museum of Indian Arts & Culture
Museum of New Mexico
710 Camino Lejo
Tel.: (505) 827-9841
Hours: Daily 10-5 (Closed Jan. & Feb.)
Admission: Yes, a 2-day pass to all museums (Museum of Fine Arts, Palace of the Governors, Museum of International Foll Art) available

27   Wheelwright Museum of the American Indian
704 Camino Lejo (behind Museum of International Folk Art)
Tel.: (505) 982-4636
Hours: Mon.-Sat. 10-5, Sun. 1-5
Admission: Donations

Page
28   Museum of International Folk Art
Museum of New Mexico
706 Camino Lejo
Tel.: (505) 827-6350
Hours: Daily 10-5 (Closed Jan. & Feb.)
Admission: Yes, a 2-day pass to all museums (Museum of Fine Arts, Palace of the Governors, Museum of Indian Arts & Culture) available

Return to Old Pecos Trail and turn left, go approximately 0.2 miles.

29   The Santa Fe Children's Museum
1050 Old Pecos Trail
Tel.: (505) 989-8359
Hours: Thurs.-Sat. 10-5, Sun. 12-5
(Closed Wednesdays during the winter)
Admission: Yes

Tour #4: OLD SPANISH RANCH

Page
36-38   El Rancho de las Golondrinas
Tel.: (505) 471-2261
Hours: Wed.-Sun. 10-4
Admission: Yes

Go Cerrillos Rd. south 7 miles (from Paseo de Peralta intersection), turn right before I-25, follow signs to race track (3.2 miles), before race track turn right, go 3.6 miles to La Cienega.

Tour #5: MISSION CHURCHES IN THE FOOTHILLS OF THE SANGRE DE CHRISTO MOUNTAINS

Page		
39	Santuario de Chimayo ♿ Tel.: (505) 351-4889 Hours: Daily 9-5:30 (winter: 9:30-4:30)	*This road is also called the High Road to Taos. You can combine it with tour #10, Taos, Taos Pueblo, Rio Grande Gorge. Take US 84-285 north to Espanola (25 miles), turn right onto NM 76 east, go 7 miles to NM 520, turn right and go 1 mile, turn left to Santuario de Chimayo.*
40	Las Trampas, San Jose de Gracias Chapel	*Return to NM 76 turn right, go 24 miles (you will pass the town of TRUCHAS where Robert Redford filmed the Milagro Beanfield War in 1986) to Las Trampas.*
41	Ranchos de Taos ♿ St. Francis of Asis Church Tel.: (505) 758-2754	*Continue on NM 76 (6 miles), turn right onto NM 75 (6.3 miles), turn left onto NM 518 (16 miles), turn left onto NM 68 to Ranchos de Taos.* *Return to Santa Fe on NM 68 (65 miles), or turn right to Taos (4 miles).*

Tour #6: HYDE MEMORIAL PARK - SF SKI BASIN AND/OR SHIDONI SCULPTURE GARDEN

Page		
42, 43	Hyde Memorial Park and Santa Fe Ski Basin Several trails within park. The Aspen Vista Road to Tesuque Peak starts at the Aspen Vista Picnic Area. The round trip hiking distance is 12 miles. Bring adequate clothing, food and water	*North on Washington Street (becomes Bishop's Lodge Road), turn right on Artist Road which becomes NM 475 (look for sign to Ski Basin after intersection with Paseo de Peralta), go 12.6 miles to Aspen View Picnic Area or 16 miles to Ski Area.*
44	Shidoni Sculpture Garden ♿ Bishop's Lodge Road, Tesuque Bronze pourings every Saturday Tel.: (505) 988-8001 Hours: Daily 9-6 Admission: Free	*North on Washington Street which becomes Bishop's Lodge Road, go 5 miles to Shidoni Sculpture Garden.*

Tour #7: OLD INDIAN RUINS

Page			
46, 47	Pecos National Monument Tel.: (505) 757-6414 Hours: Summer daily 8-6, after Labor Day 8-5 Admission: Free	♿ 🚸	*Take Old Pecos Trail south (3.3 miles), then I-25 north (16 miles). Take exit 299 (Glorieta), and follow signs (10 miles) to Pecos National Monument.*

Tour #8: TURQUOISE TRAIL TO ALBUQUERQUE

Page			
48	Cerrillos, Turquoise Mining Museum Casa Grande Trading Post Tel.: (505) 438-3008 Hours: Daily	🚸	*South on Cerrillos Road which becomes NM 14 (20 miles) to Cerrillos, Turquoise Mining Museum.*
49, 50	Madrid Old Coal Mine Museum Tel.: (505) 473-0743 Hours: Daily Admission: Yes	🚸	*Continue 4 miles south on NM 14 to Madrid.*
51	Golden Church		*Continue 10 miles on NM 14 to the Golden Church.*
52	Sandia Crest Shop and restaurant open daily year round	♿ 🚸	*Continue 11 miles to junction NM 536, turn right, go 14 miles.*
53	Albuquerque Old Town		*Return to NM 14, turn right, go 4 miles to I-40, then 17 miles to Albuquerque, exit 157A, turn left on Rio Grande Blvd. (0.5 miles) to Albuquerque Old Town.*

Tour #9: BANDELIER STATE PARK

Page			
56, 57	Bandelier National Monument Tel.: (505) 672-3861 Hours: Daily, dawn to dusk Admission: $5.00 per car	♿ 🚸	*Go US 84-285 north (16 miles), turn west on NM 502 (12.5 miles), continue on NM 4 (12 miles).*

Tour #10: TAOS BASIN - RIO GRANDE

Page			
58	Martinez Hacienda Ranchitos Road Tel.: (505) 758-1000 Hours: Daily 9-5 Admission: Yes (combination ticket available to Kit Carson House & Museum and Blumenschein Home.		*Go US 84-285 north to Espanola (26 miles), continue on NM 68 (42 miles) to Ranchos de Taos, turn left on NM 240 (4 miles).*
59	Kit Carson House & Museum East Kit Carson Road Tel.: (505) 758-4741 Hours: Daily 8-6 (Winter 9-5) Admission: Yes (combination ticket)	♿	*Continue on NM 240 (Ranchitos Rd.) for 2 miles, turn right on Camino de la Placita, then left on Paseo del Pueblo Sur (NM 68), turn right on Kit Carson Road (third house on left).*
	Blumenschein Home (not shown) Ledoux Street Tel.: (505) 758-0330 Hours: Daily 9-5 Admission: Yes (combination ticket)	♿	
60-62	Taos Pueblo Tel.: (505) 758-9593 Hours: Daily 8-5 Admission: Yes $5.00 per car, $5.00 per camera	♿	*Return to Paseo del Pueblo Norte (US 64), go 0.4 miles north, at turn go straight (2 miles) to Taos Pueblo.*
63	Millicent Rogers Museum Tel.: (505) 758-2462 Hours: Daily 9-5 Admission: Yes	♿	*Return to US 64, turn right and go 4 miles, at intersection US 64/NM 522 (Texaco gas station) make a sharp left turn and go back on unpaved road 1 mile.*
64	Rio Grande Gorge Bridge	♿	*Return to intersection 522/64, turn left onto US 64, go 7 miles.*

To return to Santa Fe you can continue on US 64 for 20 miles to Tres Piedras, then turn left onto US 285 through Carson State Park. After 22 miles either: turn right onto NM 567 and go 11 miles to the Rio Grande River (the last 3 miles down to the river are unpaved!). After the bridge, turn right and go (7 miles) along the river to Pilar where you get back onto NM 68, or continue on US 285 through Ojo Caliente, Santa Cruz, Espanola to Santa Fe (61 miles).

BOOKS BY CITIES IN COLOR, INC.

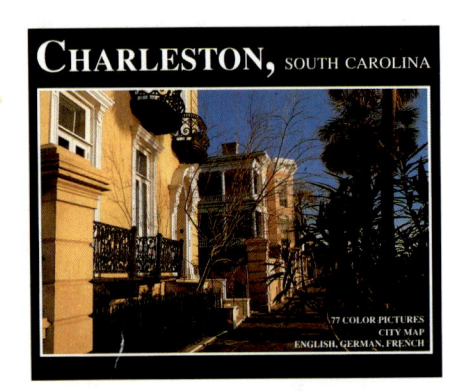

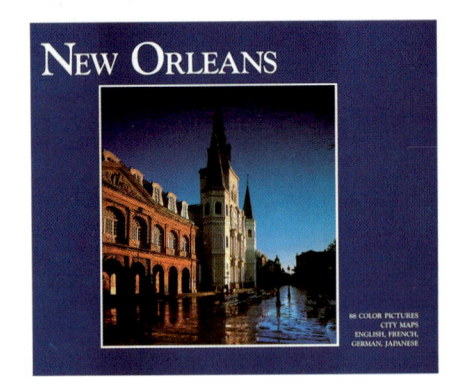

CHARLESTON, SOUTH CAROLINA
77 COLOR PICTURES
CITY MAP
ENGLISH, GERMAN, FRENCH

COLUMBIA, SOUTH CAROLINA
88 COLOR PICTURES
CITY MAP

ATLANTA

NEW ORLEANS
88 COLOR PICTURES
CITY MAPS
ENGLISH, FRENCH,
GERMAN, JAPANESE

WASHINGTON
SAVANNAH
BOSTON
To be published in 1993

Also Available:
Vienna, Austria,
Rio de Janeiro, Brazil

Cities in Color, Inc.
Lisa D. Hoff
Tel: 404 255-1185 • Fax: 404 252-7218

© CITIES IN COLOR, INC. All rights reserved.